Kristina Karlsson is the fou...
Swedish design and stationery business, kikki.K (102 kikki.k ...
stocked in another 450, and sold online to stationery and design
lovers in more than 140 countries worldwide). She's also a sought-
after international speaker, a passionate learner and self-improver
– and the proud mother of two children, Axel and Tiffany, with her
partner, Paul.

After growing up on a small farm in country Sweden, at the age of
twenty-two she found herself in a new country, half a world away
from family and friends, with little money and no idea what to do
with her life. So what was a girl to do? The answer came at 3am one
morning when she couldn't sleep and her partner, Paul, encouraged
her to write a list of everything that was important to her. The
creation of that 3am List was to be a profoundly pivotal moment in
her life, and was the inspiration for pursuing her 101 Dreams.

With deep personal experience of the power of dreaming and then
doing, Kristina is on a mission to encourage people the world over
to follow their own dreams.

Her new dream is to inspire and empower 101 million people just
like you to write their own dreams on paper and set about bringing
them to life. Why? Because by dreaming, we can all help make the
world a better place, starting with us.

Printed in China by Hung Hing Off-Set Printing Co. Ltd

ISBN 978-0-6483172-5-8

KRISTINA KARLSSON

FOLLOW
YOUR
PASSIONS

TAKE CONTROL AND START EMBRACING
MORE OF THE THINGS YOU LOVE

kikki.K

PEOPLE WITH

GREAT PASSION CAN MAKE

THE IMPOSSIBLE HAPPEN.

- ANON. -

DEDICATION

THIS BOOK IS DEDICATED TO YOU, OUR CHILDREN,
MY KIKKI.K FAMILY, AND TO THE 101 MILLION FUTURE
DREAMERS OF THE WORLD, WHOSE IMAGININGS
AND REIMAGININGS WILL SHAPE THEIR LIVES, THE
LIVES OF THEIR LOVED ONES AND THE WORLD
FOR GENERATIONS TO COME.

THANKS

A VERY BIG THANK YOU TO MY LIFE PARTNER AND
CO-CREATOR IN SO MANY WAYS, PAUL. YOU ARE TRULY
THE WIND BENEATH MY WINGS AND AS ALWAYS YOUR
CONTRIBUTION IS INSEPARABLE FROM MINE.
I LOVE OUR DREAMS.

A MASSIVE THANK YOU ALSO TO ALL THE PEOPLE
WHO HAVE LENT THEIR SUPPORT AND ALLOWED ME
TO SHARE THEIR STORIES WITH YOU IN THE PAGES AHEAD
– SO THAT TOGETHER WE CAN INSPIRE AND EMPOWER
101 MILLION PEOPLE THE WORLD OVER
TO DREAM AND DO.

IF IT EXCITES YOU,

IF IT SCARES YOU, IF IT

MOVES YOU, GO AND DO IT!

CONTENTS

HOW TO GET THE MOST VALUE
FROM THIS BOOK

I recommend that you approach this book step by step. Read each chapter thoroughly. Re-read it if you need to. Then do the exercises at the end of each chapter before moving to the next.

Take your time. We're all so different, but my estimate is that on average each chapter will take you about an hour to complete – including the reading and doing. Some may take longer, all depending on how deeply you challenge yourself and the pace you want to go at.

My experience is that doing work on yourself like this prompts lots of thoughts and ideas for days afterwards, giving you the chance to refine things as you think about them. I came up with my 3am List of things that really mattered to me at – no surprises – 3am one sleepless night. But my list of 101 Dreams took much longer – in fact, I continue to work on and refine it as a regular practice. And trust me, it's worth it!

Consider involving your partner, other family members or like-minded friends or colleagues in the process of reading and working through this book – and even some of the exercises. I've found it so rewarding – and fun – to work with others on my practice of dreaming and visualisation over the years.

Let this book inspire you to dream big, write down those dreams and start taking action to bring them to life. And don't forget, you can join our global community and discover a world of inspiration and further dreaming guidance, including my *Your Dream Life Starts Here* book and journal, my 'Your Dream Life with Kristina Karlsson' podcast, workshops, free audio guides, worksheets and more, at www.kikki-k.com/dreamlife.

WHERE TO DO
THE WRITTEN EXERCISES

Putting pen to paper and working through the exercises at the end of each chapter is where you will get the most value from this book. Reading is one way of learning, but absorbing yourself in doing the exercises will take you to a whole new level.

You will find the exercises stimulating, fun, challenging and sometimes perhaps confronting. But your dream life lies somewhere beyond your comfort zone.

A good option is to use a new journal or notebook to do the exercises. Make sure it has plenty of pages so you can keep all your work in the one place – easy to find when you need it and to look back on.

WHAT'S YOUR PASSION?

Something magical happens when you find your true passions in life. Something even more powerful happens when you draw on your passions as stepping stones to create the life of your dreams – it's a life-changing process.

But few of us enter adulthood knowing how to harness our passions and embrace the power of dreaming. Even fewer venture past merely wishing and hoping into purposefully pursuing our passions. Instead, many of us drift or race through our days, settling for the ordinary or just trying to survive, when we could be seizing the opportunity of each precious new day to create and live our dream lives. We live our lives without the passion they could have.

This is what I want to change. My promise to you is that if you seize hold of your passions, your dream life truly can start here – if you want it to and if you take responsibility for making it happen.

My theory is that the only reason people don't consistently practise dreaming in their lives is because they haven't been taught how. I want to change that by sharing the message far and wide, and inspiring the world to dream.

If you have ever wanted something more from life, something different, but not known where to begin, this book is for you. It's filled with powerful ideas and simple proven tools that will help you discover your passions and transform your dreams into a life designed by you for you, and for your loved ones.

In this book you'll read the inspiring stories and wisdom of people like Arianna Huffington and Li Cunxin (*Mao's Last Dancer*) that will show you how to harness your passions and the power of dreaming to genuinely transform your life. I've also talked to some amazing people about how they discovered their passions in life for my podcast 'Your Dream Life with Kristina Karlsson'. Listen and subscribe on Apple Podcasts, Google Podcasts or your preferred podcast streaming app.

Life is short and you deserve to spend as much of it doing things you are passionate about – that spark joy and give you a sense of meaning. What happens next is up to you – but be prepared for an amazing adventure!

DREAM GUIDANCE

To help you get started, here is what I share with people about dreaming – which really helped me as a first step to discovering what I was really passionate about. This powerful exercise will show you how to practise dreaming completely without limitations. If you've already done this exercise and want to get straight into the guidance and exercises in this book, go to page 19.

When I first discovered this practice, I wrote down a list of everything that bubbled up for me. They were big dreams, far beyond my normal thinking, and it was so exciting to see them take shape on paper – almost as if they had a life of their own. I encourage you to do this exercise often – aim for 101 Dreams if you can! To capture your dreams, start a 101 Dreams List in your notebook or journal (or add them to an existing list you may have started already). The exercises in this book will help you discover what you are truly passionate about, which, in turn, will help to inspire many more dreams!

Read through this guidance as many times as you like as you do this practice. A good alternative is to listen to my 101 Dreams Guide as you write – many people find the verbal prompts, inspiration and guidance help them get the most from the experience and it's really useful to play in the background if you're dreaming with others (www.kikki-k.com/bookresources).

And for further inspiration, read the various dreams we've assembled on the following pages – they're from my kikki.K team and their families, our guests (that's what we call our customers), people I know, some of the many people I meet around the world who share their dreams with me and others. Some of them shared anonymously. If any of them inspire ideas for dreams for you, then add them to your 101 Dreams List.

To begin, immerse yourself in your inspiring space where you won't be interrupted. When you're ready, close your eyes while you take three slow, deep breaths. This is your time. Open your eyes when you're done.

Don't worry about the doing. Don't filter what you come up with. Don't worry about sorting through them. Just connect with your heart, dream big and capture those dreams on paper as quickly, roughly and simply as you like. Think of this as a brainstorming exercise.

I want you to imagine your life without any limitations. You have all the money you need. Time is no limit. There is no urgency. No musts. No shoulds. And you cannot fail.

Imagine you can do whatever you want to do and have whatever you want to have. To be whoever you want to be.

You are not constrained at all by what your parents think, what your friends think, what your partner thinks, what anyone thinks. You are totally free to just be you – to be your best self and to dream without any limitations about what you want for yourself, for those you love and care about, and for the world.

I'm giving you permission to stop for a moment and just let go of everything you thought you could or couldn't do. The world is so full of possibilities. It all starts with a dream, so this is your turn to cast all doubts and all constraints aside and give yourself the gift of dreaming. Dream away.

Afterwards, put pen to paper and use the below two questions to inspire, prompt and guide you to create your list of 101 Dreams – or as many as you can.

+ *WHAT WOULD YOU DO IF YOU KNEW YOU COULD NOT FAIL?*
+ *WHAT WOULD YOU DO IF YOU HAD ALL THE MONEY AND TIME YOU NEEDED?*

+ *'A dream of mine is to dance with my daughter at her wedding. I might be in my seventies by then so I need to be healthy, fit and agile!'* – Paul, 50

+ *'My BIG Dream is to create gourmet home-cooked meals for dogs and deliver fresh, wholesome meals to pet lovers all over my local area.'* – Misty

+ *'My dream is to make a living vlogging on YouTube.'* – Axel (axelkl), 10

+ *'My dream is to be a career consultant for young women. I want to help them recognise their passion, power and talents so they make the best career choices that they can.'* – Marin

+ *'My dream is to nurse in a paediatric hospital on Christmas Day, to make the day exceptionally special and make children smile through a difficult time.'*

+ *'To grow my business to a point where I feel fulfilled and have enough money to spoil my family and thank them for all they have done for me.'*

+ *'Open a retreat on my five-acre farm specifically for families going through hardship with their children in hospital (a home away from home) just as we did staying at Ronald McDonald House when our twins had heart surgeries.'* – Rebecca

+ *'My dream is simple. To own my story, to be in the driving seat of my own life. To overcome the things holding me back.'*

+ *'My dream is to complete the four-part book series I've been working on since 1999 based on music my sister wrote for piano. I am currently half way through book three.'* – Jason

+ *'I have a dream where all humans are treated equally – in love, in respect, in wealth, in health, etc. – no matter where they're from. Who knows, we might not be the only humans in the universe.'* – Robert

+ *'My dream is to one day dance for the National Ballet. Just being able to perform and call myself a member of the company would be a dream come true.'*

+ *'To create regular space in our lives where my husband and I can spend quality time together without the rush and demands of everyday life.'*

+ *'I'm dreaming of opening my own café – healthy food and great coffee.'*

+ *'Take a year off and travel the world – and learn what I can about how we can solve our many environmental challenges.'*

IF YOU'RE NOT HAPPY

WITH THE DIRECTION

YOUR LIFE IS GOING,

MAKE A TURN.

1

YOU'RE IN THE DRIVER'S SEAT

FOLLOW YOUR PASSIONS

YOUR

DREAM LIFE

IS POSSIBLE.

Before we get deeper into exploring and discovering your passions, I want you to know something important. Something that's essential to the work we'll do together.

**YOU ARE IN CONTROL OF YOUR OWN LIFE.
IT'S YOU IN THE DRIVER'S SEAT.**

Right now, you have everything you need to imagine the life you want to live and to transform yourself in whatever way you want. It's up to you to embrace your passions and make your dream life happen – to take control of your own personal growth and your experience of life. You don't need to wait for anyone or anything else to change or be different.

'YOU ARE ENTIRELY UP TO YOU.'

- ANON. -

Now does this idea excite and inspire you, or scare you? Take note of the feeling – maybe even scribble it in the space on the side of this paragraph. One day you'll be able to look back and remember exactly how you felt today.

You may already know and embrace this concept and maybe that's just how you live your life. If so, well done. I meet so many people who share with me that they can't see, for various reasons, how they can take control of their life. Or they understand the concept, but struggle to really embrace it at important moments.

After years of learning from experience and immersing myself in personal development material, I have absorbed so much. One of the most important lessons for me has been that – regardless of your education or circumstances – *you and only you can change your own life.*

As a teenager, I remember thinking that if my circumstances were different – if I had more knowledge, more experience, more money, if I had more education or lived in a big city – then my life would be better, more exciting and easier...

Looking back, it's clear that as a young girl I believed that external factors held more sway over my destiny than I did. I didn't stop to think about what *I* could do to make my life better. The 3am moment when I first came up with a list of things I was passionate about was the turning point for me. Taking full control of my life for the first time was an indescribable, exciting feeling.

It's funny how many people think kikki.K was an overnight success story. If only. When I first started kikki.K, I quite literally lived on soup – it was cheap, healthy and I could save lots of time by cooking a big batch twice a week instead of cooking daily.

I worked breakfast and night shifts in hospitality so that I could spend my days working unpaid on my business dream. I borrowed $3,000 from my partner, Paul, to design and produce my first range of colour-matching folders, notebooks and storage boxes. Then I'd fill my car to overflowing with products (usually with the last box on my lap!) and drive to friends' homes to share my dream for kikki.K and offer my first products for sale. I maxed out every credit card I could get my hands on until I convinced Paul to sell his house so we could fund the launch of our very first kikki.K store – and yes, he's very grateful he did!

I did whatever I could to make it work because I knew it was up to me to do so. If I didn't take responsibility, then why would anyone else? This was my passion, my dream, and I was in the driver's seat.

WHETHER YOU WANT TO...

+ START YOUR OWN BUSINESS

+ LAND A GREAT JOB OR GET PROMOTED

+ TAKE A SABBATICAL

+ CLIMB MOUNT EVEREST

+ MASTER A NEW LANGUAGE

+ BE THE BEST PARENT YOU CAN BE

+ BECOME A LEADER IN YOUR COMMUNITY

+ GRADUATE WITH A DEGREE

+ RAISE CHILDREN WHO WILL MAKE A DIFFERENCE IN THE WORLD

+ TAKE YOUR TALENT TO THE NEXT LEVEL

+ MAKE A LIVING FROM YOUR PASSION

+ WORK OUT WHAT'S NEXT FOR YOU AFTER YOUR CHILDREN HAVE
  LEFT HOME

...IT'S UP TO *YOU*

FOR ANOTHER INSPIRING EXAMPLE OF HOW, BY JUMPING IN THE DRIVER'S SEAT AND TAKING CONTROL, YOU CAN CREATE A HAPPIER LIFE – YOUR DREAM LIFE – BE SURE TO LISTEN TO THE INCREDIBLE CONVERSATION I HAD WITH GRETCHEN RUBIN, MULTIPLE *NEW YORK TIMES* BESTSELLING AUTHOR OF *THE HAPPINESS PROJECT*, *BETTER THAN BEFORE* AND *OUTER ORDER, INNER CALM*, ON MY PODCAST – 'YOUR DREAM LIFE WITH KRISTINA KARLSSON'. LISTEN TO HER INCREDIBLE EPISODE AND SUBSCRIBE ON APPLE PODCASTS, GOOGLE PODCASTS OR YOUR PREFERRED PODCAST STREAMING APP.

YOU HAVE BRAINS IN YOUR HEAD.

YOU HAVE FEET IN YOUR SHOES.

YOU CAN STEER YOURSELF ANY

DIRECTION YOU CHOOSE.

YOU'RE ON YOUR OWN. AND YOU

KNOW WHAT YOU KNOW.

AND YOU'RE THE ONE WHO'LL

DECIDE WHERE TO GO…

- DR SEUSS, *OH, THE PLACES YOU'LL GO!* -

YOU HAVE EVERYTHING YOU NEED TO MAKE THE NECESSARY DECISIONS ALONG THE PATHWAY TO YOUR DREAM LIFE.

You can decide right now to change habits, to start something new or go after a goal. Or you can do the complete opposite. And it really doesn't matter what you choose, so long as you're happy with those decisions.

So my questions for you to now contemplate and answer in your notebook or journal are:

01 /

THINK OF SOMEONE YOU KNOW WHO STEERS THEIR JOURNEY THROUGH
LIFE FROM THE DRIVER'S SEAT. WHAT DO YOU ADMIRE MOST ABOUT THEM?
WHAT COULD YOU LEARN FROM THEM AND USE IN CREATING YOUR OWN
DREAM LIFE?

---

02 /

WHAT ARE THREE KEY THINGS THAT HAVE HAPPENED IN THE LAST FEW
YEARS THAT HAVE LED YOU TO WHERE YOU ARE TODAY?

---

03 /

FOR EACH, HOW MUCH WAS DRIVEN BY YOU? HOW MUCH WAS DRIVEN BY
OTHER PEOPLE OR CIRCUMSTANCES BEYOND YOUR CONTROL? HOW DO YOU
FEEL ABOUT THAT?

---

04 /

WHAT DO YOU NEED TO START DOING TO TAKE BETTER CONTROL OF YOUR
LIFE? IN FACT, WHAT ARE THREE CHOICES THAT YOU CAN MAKE THIS WEEK
THAT WILL GET YOU CLOSER TO YOUR DREAM LIFE NOW?

05 /

WHAT DO YOU NEED TO STOP DOING? WHAT IS NOT SERVING YOU WELL
(FOR EXAMPLE, SAYING YES WHEN YOU REALLY WANT TO SAY NO)?

---

06 /

HOW STRONGLY DO YOU BELIEVE IN YOUR ABILITY TO TURN DREAMS INTO
REALITY? (THIS IS A FUN QUESTION TO REVISIT IN A YEAR'S TIME, ONCE
YOU'VE HAD TIME TO PRACTISE.)

---

07 /

KNOWING THAT HOW YOU FEEL EACH DAY IS ACTUALLY YOUR CHOICE, THINK
ABOUT TO WHAT DEGREE THE WAY YOU LIVE YOUR LIFE NOW BRINGS YOU
JOY. DO YOU WAKE UP EXCITED FOR THE DAY? HOW DO YOU WANT TO FEEL
EACH DAY? WHAT THREE THINGS WILL YOU DO TO MAKE THAT FEELING A
REALITY?

---

08 /

THINK ABOUT THE ANSWERS YOU'VE WRITTEN TO THE QUESTIONS ABOVE.
DO ANY OF THEM PROMPT ANYTHING FOR YOU THAT YOU WANT TO ADD TO
YOUR LIST OF 101 DREAMS? GO DO IT...

WHO YOU ARE TOMORROW BEGINS

WITH WHAT YOU DO TODAY.

- TIM FARGO -

YOU'RE IN THE DRIVER'S SEAT

1
YOU ARE IN THE DRIVER'S
SEAT OF YOUR OWN LIFE

2
YOU HAVE THE POWER TO
CREATE CHANGE IF YOU
WANT TO

3
IF YOU WANT TO CREATE
CHANGE, YOU HAVE TO
BELIEVE IN YOURSELF!

I AM NOT A PRODUCT OF

MY CIRCUMSTANCES.

I AM A PRODUCT OF

MY DECISIONS.

- STEPHEN COVEY -

'YOU ARE IN CONTROL
OF THE CLICKER.'

ARIANNA HUFFINGTON

Arianna Huffington is such an inspiring woman. I first met her after reading her book *Thrive: The Third Metric to Redefining Success and Creating a Life of Well-Being, Wisdom, and Wonder*,[1] which I found so inspiring that I chased around after her to see if she wanted to collaborate to create a Thrive Collection for kikki.K so we could share the messages we both believe in more widely across the world. She did, and so that's what we did.

To the world, she's a Greek-American author, syndicated columnist and highly successful businesswoman, not to mention the co-founder and former Editor-in-Chief of *The Huffington Post* (which is now owned by AOL). To me, she's a friend and sometimes mentor – no fuss, straight shooter – and I cherish the times we get to catch up when our busy paths cross.

In 2009, Arianna was ranked twelfth in *Forbes'* first-ever list of the 'Most Influential Women in Media'. In 2014, she was listed by *Forbes* as the fifty-second 'Most Powerful Woman in the World'. Both achievements are a far cry from her humble childhood beginnings.

---

1 ARIANNA HUFFINGTON, *THE THIRD METRIC TO REDEFINING SUCCESS AND CREATING A LIFE OF WELL-BEING, WISDOM, AND WONDER* (NEW YORK: HARMONY BOOKS, 2014)

There is so much inspiration to be drawn from Arianna's life – and I urge you to read her books and research her story for yourself – but I learnt two key things from her story. Simple things, but so very valuable, and I want to focus you on them both to help you take hold of your passions. First, that looking at the world with a sense of wonder, no matter what life throws at you, is a brilliant attitude to cultivate. Second, that we are all in the drivers' seats of our own lives.

In her book *Thrive*, Arianna explains how one of the gifts her mother passed on to her was her sense of curiosity and wonder.

'Countless things in our daily lives can awaken the almost constant state of wonder we knew as children,' says Arianna, '...but sometimes to see them we must look through a different set of eyes.'

Taking time out to consciously dream – to open your heart and truly follow your passions – is one highly valuable way for you to look at the world through a different set of eyes. Take inspiration from Arianna and bring that into your life.

Whenever Arianna was upset or would complain about something, her mother would say, 'Just change the channel. You are in control of the clicker. Don't replay the bad, scary movie.' This sound advice has served Arianna well – she's someone clearly in the driver's seat of her own life, who chooses to focus on solutions rather than complaining about problems, which has helped her inspire millions through her books, businesses and media appearances.

Another gem from Arianna's story that I love is her view that it's not 'What do I want to do?', it's 'What kind of life do I want to live?' A woman truly after my own heart, Arianna is living proof that it's possible, if you want, to dream up and create a dream life for you and your loved ones.

Let Arianna's story inspire you to take control of your life. Take some time now while it's fresh in your mind to think about it and write down anything you've learnt that you could apply in your own life in your notebook or journal.

I ALSO ENCOURAGE YOU TO LISTEN TO MY CONVERSATION WITH ARIANNA ON MY PODCAST 'YOUR DREAM LIFE WITH KRISTINA KARLSSON'. IN THE EPISODE, ARIANNA DISCUSSES HOW TO CREATE A LIFE YOU TRULY LOVE BY GETTING IN TOUCH WITH WHAT YOU REALLY WANT (NOT WHAT SOMEONE ELSE WANTS FOR YOU). SUBSCRIBE ON APPLE PODCASTS, GOOGLE PODCASTS OR YOUR PREFERRED PODCAST STREAMING APP.

ANYTHING THAT GETS YOUR

BLOOD RACING IS PROBABLY

WORTH DOING.

- HUNTER S. THOMPSON -

THE ONLY THING THAT WILL

STOP YOU FROM FULFILLING

YOUR DREAMS IS YOU.

- TOM BRADLEY -

2

WHO ARE YOU AND WHERE ARE YOU AT RIGHT NOW?

FOLLOW YOUR PASSIONS

AWARENESS IS THE GREATEST

AGENT FOR CHANGE.

- ECKHART TOLLE -

Being an avid reader of everything I can lay my hands on in the personal development space, I'm constantly inspired to improve my life. I write notes and ideas in my journal every day and, over the years, I've learnt that you need to know where you are before you can decide where you want to go. And how you will get there. It's also a key step before we dive deeper into discovering and following your passions.

Think about your current circumstances. Where are you at right now? And what brought you to this place? To start taking steps to living your dream life, you need knowledge of yourself and an awareness of the journey you've already taken, including decisions you have made along the way that have brought you to where you are today.

When I look back over my life, I can identify a number of important moments when I've made big decisions or experienced events that changed the course of my life and shaped the person I am today.

Deciding to move to Melbourne from Sweden and start a new life in a new country was one of those moments. Deciding to start my own business and launch kikki.K was another. Others include supporting my younger brother, Hans, through serious illness, deciding to become a mother and, just recently, taking the decision to live in Sweden for a year with our two young children, which had long been a family dream. Being asked to speak publicly and choosing to do that was a pivotal moment too – it was one thing I really feared – and while I still don't love it, I do love sharing my experiences with others and seeing how that inspires people.

When I think about decisive moments like these, I remember feeling both terrified and excited at the same time. Oddly enough, I've grown to *love* that feeling. It's when I know I'm doing something that matters, something that will push me and help me grow. That feeling is a great sign that you're moving out of your comfort zone and towards your dream life.

Looking back over your own life, you'll recognise that you've achieved so much already and it's those moments that can inspire you to push even further and dream even bigger. Our life stories make us who we are – and they influence our view of the future. Our dreams.

One of my favourite quotes is by Aristotle:

'KNOWING YOURSELF IS THE BEGINNING OF ALL WISDOM.'

I love these words. The more self-awareness you have and the more you know yourself, the more you're able to understand why you make certain decisions, why you form certain habits and, importantly, what makes you feel your best.

If you know these things, you can learn what you need to make time for and how to live your best life. Self-awareness is about being honest with yourself and looking at your life without judgement. It's about understanding what your strengths and weaknesses are at any given point in your life, what influences your decisions, and whether your attitude and mindset is serving you or holding you back. It's also about understanding the choices you make, without feeling guilty or ashamed if you fall short of your ideal.

You might find the process of looking deep into yourself a little confronting and challenging. That's a good thing. When you're out of your comfort zone, you know you're growing personally. Stick with me here and trust me that it's worth doing this well.

A few years ago, after a session reflecting on where I was at, I had been wrestling with why it was so difficult to get out of bed early in the mornings. I love mornings, but I'd slipped into a pattern of not sleeping well, which made it hard to rise and shine when I wanted to. Through that process of self-reflection, I realised that the couple of glasses of wine I was having with dinner during the week was probably affecting my ability to sleep well, which was making it hard for me to get up and do the exercise and other things I wanted to do in the early morning.

That led me to challenge myself to give up alcohol and sugar for three months to see if I could sleep better. I *did* sleep better. And it did help me get up earlier and exercise, which in turn helped me feel more energetic and creative, and get more done. The experience taught me some good lessons about balancing my life.

ACCEPT YOURSELF AS YOU ARE, WHILE ALWAYS STRIVING TO BE BETTER AND IMAGINING THE FUTURE YOU WANT TO CREATE.

Something I do at the end of every year is to answer the list of questions at the end of this chapter. This helps me understand who I am and where I'm at, at this particular point in time (remembering that we're all always evolving). It's a great place to start before deciding where I want to go in the next twelve months and what dreams I want to chase.

I have a dream that I never want to live the same year twice. I always want to add something different to the new year ahead. This makes me carefully look through my list of dreams each year and intentionally choose to focus on adding something new to my life. I love thinking and pondering what this can be as I reflect on where I am in life at my annual check-in.

I usually do this in November or December when I'm starting to set goals and plan for the new year, but you can do it whenever you choose. I always have my previous journals and diary handy, to glance through and remind myself just how much I managed to squeeze in over the preceding year. It's a beautiful, feel-good exercise and something I always anticipate eagerly.

Work through the below questions. Jot down your answers and reflect on them afterwards. Keep your answers somewhere safe so that you can revisit them next year or whenever you need.

01 /

REFLECT AND WRITE DOWN YOUR ANSWERS TO:

+ TEN WONDERFUL THINGS THAT HAPPENED IN THE LAST TWELVE MONTHS

+ FIVE THINGS I'M MOST PROUD OF FROM THE LAST TWELVE MONTHS

+ FIVE LESSONS I LEARNT IN THE LAST TWELVE MONTHS

+ FIVE THINGS I WANT TO DO LESS OF, OR NOT AT ALL, IN THE NEXT TWELVE MONTHS

+ FIVE THINGS I WANT TO DO MORE OF IN THE NEXT TWELVE MONTHS

+ FIVE THINGS I'M GRATEFUL FOR IN THE LAST TWELVE MONTHS

+ FIVE THINGS I DID THAT TOOK ME CLOSER TO LIVING MY DREAM LIFE IN THE LAST TWELVE MONTHS

+ FIVE THINGS I WANT TO DO TO IMPROVE MY LIFE

+ FIVE GREAT DECISIONS I MADE IN THE LAST TWELVE MONTHS

+ IF I COULD LIVE THE LAST TWELVE MONTHS AGAIN, WHAT WOULD I CHANGE AND WHY?

02 /

REFLECT AT A HIGH LEVEL ON THE FOLLOWING AREAS OF YOUR LIFE AND
GIVE YOURSELF A RATING OUT OF TEN FOR EACH (WITH 10 BEING 'I'M
COMPLETELY SATISFIED WITH MY LIFE IN THIS AREA' AND 1 BEING 'I'M
COMPLETELY UNSATISFIED WITH MY LIFE IN THIS AREA'). THIS WILL HELP
GIVE YOU A CLEARER INDICATION OF WHERE YOU ARE AT RIGHT NOW.

+ CAREER AND FINANCES
+ EDUCATION AND LEARNING
+ HEALTH, WELLNESS AND FITNESS
+ FAMILY AND RELATIONSHIPS
+ HOME
+ SPIRITUALITY AND/OR SENSE OF PURPOSE
+ TRAVEL AND EXPERIENCES
+ HOBBIES/FUN
+ COMMUNITY AND ENVIRONMENT

---

03 /

NOW, NEXT TO EACH RATING, USE A DIFFERENT COLOURED PEN TO
INDICATE WHERE YOU WOULD LIKE TO BE FOR EACH CATEGORY. YOU
MAY SET THE BAR HIGHER, LOWER OR EVEN LEAVE IT EXACTLY AS IT IS
TODAY. REMEMBER, THIS IS JUST A VERY HIGH-LEVEL EXERCISE TO GET
YOU THINKING.

I'M A BIG BELIEVER IN THE FACT THAT YOU CAN DO ANYTHING – JUST NOT
EVERYTHING AT THE SAME TIME. IN MY OWN LIFE, I CUT BACK ON PUBLIC
SPEAKING AND WORK AFTER THE BIRTH OF MY CHILDREN, KNOWING THAT I
REALLY WANTED TO FOCUS MORE ON FAMILY, ONE OF MY CORE VALUES.

MAYBE THIS YEAR YOU WILL CHOOSE TO FOCUS ON JUST ONE OR TWO KEY
AREAS, AND THAT'S FINE. WHAT'S MOST IMPORTANT IS GETTING A CLEAR
IDEA OF WHERE YOU WANT TO BE. AND THIS IS THE EXCITING PART!

04 /

REFLECT ON WHAT THIS EXERCISE IS TELLING YOU. DOES IT REVEAL
ANYTHING ABOUT WHAT YOUR PRIORITIES SHOULD BE FOR THE NEXT
TWELVE MONTHS? MAKE A NOTE, AND I ENCOURAGE YOU TO REFLECT AND
COMPLETE THIS EXERCISE AGAIN IN TWELVE MONTHS. PUT A REMINDER IN
YOUR DIARY.

---

05 /

REFLECT ON WHETHER ANYTHING FROM THIS EXERCISE HAS TRIGGERED
ANY DREAMS TO BE ADDED TO YOUR 101 DREAMS LIST, AND THEN GO
ADD THEM.

ONLY WHEN WE ARE BRAVE ENOUGH

TO EXPLORE OUR DARKNESS WILL

WE DISCOVER THE INFINITE POWER

OF OUR LIGHT.

- BRENÉ BROWN -

WHO ARE YOU AND WHERE ARE YOU AT RIGHT NOW?

1

THE MORE SELF-AWARE YOU ARE, THE BETTER YOU CAN ADAPT AND GROW

2

THE MORE YOU CAN ADAPT AND GROW, THE BETTER YOU CAN LIVE YOUR DREAM LIFE

3

YOU CAN GROW YOUR SELF-AWARENESS THROUGH REFLECTION, JOURNALING AND LEARNING

'I THOUGHT AGAIN OF THE LITTLE FROG IN THE WELL...'

LI CUNXIN

I will never forget having the honour of hearing Li Cunxin tell his life story first-hand. How he survived a childhood of bitter poverty and, inspired by his dreams, became one of the world's best male ballet dancers. Not an eye in the room was dry and we all left that day incredibly inspired and grateful for the many learnings we had made about the power of dreams ... and how to make them come true.

I subsequently read his autobiography, *Mao's Last Dancer*,[2] watched the feature film adapted from this book when it came out in 2009 and after stumbling upon his children's book, *The Peasant Prince*,[3] have read that many times to my children. They love it and we've spent many hours talking about the inspiration we all draw from his story. You really must read his books and watch the movie.

Li grew up in bitter poverty near the city of Qingdao, in Shandong province in north-east China. Born in 1961, the sixth of seven brothers, into a poor rural family, his childhood coincided with a period in China's history when food was scarce for millions.

2   LI CUNXIN, *MAO'S LAST DANCER* (MELBOURNE: PENGUIN VIKING, 2003)
3   LI CUNXIN, *THE PEASANT PRINCE* (MELBOURNE: PENGUIN VIKING, 2007)

Li recalls: 'When we all sat down to eat, we would stare longingly at what little food there was. Every night our mother would pray that none of her sons would die from starvation. I was always hungry.'

One of the most compelling elements of his life story for me was his very clear memory of a story that his father told him many times as a child, his fascination with that story and the way that story inspired him to dream.

The story was about a frog that lived at the bottom of a deep, dark well from which there was no chance of escape to the bigger, better world above. It was clear his father was referencing the poor circumstances in which the family lived – stuck in poverty – and, like the little frog, their slim chance of escaping.

But the way his father told the story gave Li hope and fuelled his childhood dreams to one day help his family escape the poverty they were all trapped in.

Li's father recounted in his story that despite the frog's father telling the little frog 'there is no way you can get out of here ... I've tried all my life ... forget the world above', the little frog still 'spent his life trying to escape the cold, dark well'. The tale gave Li hope, helped him cope with monumental challenges, and fuelled his dream to escape poverty and to help his family.

'I thought about that poor frog in the well many times,' says Li. And he recalls the story affecting him so strongly as a young child that he would attach three dreams to his kite and fly them as 'messages to the gods'. 'My first wish was for my mother's happiness and long life. My second wish was for my father's happiness and long life. My third wish was to get out of the deep dark well. I dreamed about all the beautiful things in life that were not mine. Food for my family. I begged the gods to get me out of the well so I could help my family.'

Li was linking his dreams to the betterment of others – his family – and he was instinctively giving his dreams symbolic importance, bringing them to life by tying them to his kite and flying them up into the sky.

Things took a turn when Li was eleven. He recalls: 'One very cold day, four strange officials came into our classroom. They wanted to take some children to study something called ballet. Only one girl was chosen from my class. Then, just as they were about to leave, Teacher Song suddenly pointed at me. "What about that one?" she said. "Okay, he can come too," was the answer.' It was a moment that, by the thinnest thread of chance, changed the course of his life.

He joined a group of about ten other children from other classes that day who were all measured and tested. 'My legs were lifted high, my body was stretched,' he remembers. 'Other children cried out in pain, but I did not. I thought again of the little frog in the well. Perhaps if I could pass this test I could help my family live a better life.' Li's dream had been the driving force for him to summon his courage and find a way to turn this stroke of luck into the opportunity of a lifetime.

For many weeks he waited. Then came the exciting news! Li Cunxin, a poor peasant boy, had been chosen from millions of children in the whole of China. He was to leave home and become a dancer. He remembers his mother saying to him, 'My dear son, this is your one chance to escape this cruel world. You have your secret dreams. Follow them! Make them come true!' And he did.

Li struggled at first with ballet and a harsh regime that included a gruelling sixteen hours a day of training, starting each morning at 5:30am. He also recalls being desperately sad at being separated from his beloved family at such a young age, and crying himself to sleep most nights.

However, through great courage, determination and hard work – driven by dreams of helping his family one day and with the guidance of a teacher named Xiao – by the end of the seven-year training he had become a very good dancer. One of China's best.

He was one of the first students from the Beijing Dance Academy to go to the United States on a scholarship to dance with the Houston Ballet in 1979, and famously created headlines when he defected to the West. This resulted in his Chinese citizenship being revoked. As a result, he was cut off from his beloved family for nine years, before eventually being able to fulfil his dream of helping them out of poverty. He remembers with excitement when he was finally allowed back into China in June 1988, returning home with five suitcases full of gifts and buying two much-needed refrigerators for his family.

Li danced with the Houston Ballet for sixteen years, achieving the rank of Principal in 1982. He won many awards and accolades, including two silver medals and one bronze medal at three international ballet competitions and two highly prestigious Princess Grace Awards, in the process becoming one of the world's best male ballet dancers.

There is so much more to his remarkable story, a story that demonstrates that it's possible to rise from even the most awful circumstances if you have a dream, if it's strong enough, if you believe in it and if you work hard. Despite enormous obstacles, Li's dreams pulled him forwards and opened him up to possibility, preparing him for those moments in his life when opportunities presented themselves.

Li fell in love with Australian dancer, Mary McKendry, a Principal Dancer with the Houston Ballet, and eventually made his way to settle and start a family in Melbourne, Australia. He turned his hand to finance after his dancing career, building a successful and lucrative career as a stockbroker before giving it up to again follow his passion for the art form of ballet. He is now the Artistic Director of Queensland Ballet – a vibrant, creative and world-class company – where his purpose has turned to helping others make their dreams come true through ballet. His dreams are truly tied to the dreams of others.

Let Li's amazing story inspire you to dream big for yourself and your loved ones. Take some time now while it's fresh in your mind to ponder on it and write down anything you've learnt that you could apply in your own life in your notebook or journal.

A DREAM WITHOUT A PLAN

IS JUST A WISH.

- KATHERINE PATERSON -

DON'T ASK WHAT THE WORLD

NEEDS. ASK WHAT MAKES

YOU COME ALIVE, AND GO

DO IT. BECAUSE WHAT

THE WORLD NEEDS IS PEOPLE

WHO HAVE COME ALIVE.

- HOWARD THURMAN -

3

DISCOVER AND FOLLOW
YOUR PASSIONS

FOLLOW YOUR PASSIONS

OUR PASSION

IS OUR STRENGTH.

- BILLIE JOE ARMSTRONG -

Imagine what it would be like to spend most of your time doing things you don't like, in an environment you don't like, surrounded by people you don't like. Not much fun?

In my experience, the answer to avoiding this trap has been to follow my passions – to spend as much time as possible doing things that I love and that make me feel truly alive. For me, because I realised that in life we usually need to spend a lot of time working, I decided that combining work and my passions made sense.

When your work involves something you care deeply about, then you have the chance to live and breathe your passion. For example, I started doing Arianna's online *Thrive* course out of personal interest, but this soon blurred into work as I loved it so much that we ended up doing a collaboration with her. Lots of my big ideas come when I'm doing a course, reading or simply out walking. It's then I feel as if my life, work and purpose go hand in hand. It simply doesn't feel like I'm working – more like I'm living my purpose. You deserve to have that feeling too.

That does not mean that life then becomes a breeze. Even when you follow your passions, there are ups and downs, and things you need to do that are less enjoyable than others. But if you are pursuing a dream you are passionate about, you will never be too far away from things that you really value and love. Understanding and being deep in financials helps me run my business better, so I can see its inherent value, even though it's certainly not as close to my heart as, say, design.

So ... when people ask me, as they often do, 'What is the number one thing to know about starting a business?', I always answer: 'Find something you're passionate about.'

I give the same answer when people tell me they don't enjoy their jobs. And this doesn't just apply to starting a business or to finding a career you love – I believe it applies to *anything* you want to do in life. Life is short and you deserve to spend as much of your precious time doing things you are passionate about, that give you a sense of meaning and joy, and which bring you into regular contact with like-minded people. Seriously, you deserve this.

The wonderful news is that you have a choice. You are in the driver's seat. You can choose to find and follow passions and you can also choose to move away from things you don't love – things that sap your spirit rather than giving you energy and joy. That's worth reflecting on.

Many people tell me it's not so easy finding things to feel passionate about. So we're going to do some thinking and exercises to explore and help get you closer to finding out what your true passions are.

I do these exercises every year and recommend you do them yearly too. Over time, we all grow and change, as do our priorities and interests, so it's worth checking in annually on this.

When I was searching for my 'thing' – my passion – kikki.K wasn't the first option I explored. When I was still at school, and trying to figure out what I wanted to do when I finished, for some reason optometry came to mind. Then I discovered that it's a very hard course to get into in Sweden, so I'd have to work very hard to get the necessary marks.

That's when I decided it might first be a good idea to see what being an optometrist was really like. I contacted the local optometrist in my hometown of Falkenberg, Sweden, and asked if I could work for free every Thursday afternoon in return for the opportunity to learn more about optometry as a career.

A couple of months were enough for me to know that glasses and eyes were *not* my destiny. I was very grateful that I found out so quickly, rather than after years of study. So I continued my search, but without knowing what I know today about dreaming – and am sharing here with you – I was still feeling my way.

IF ONLY ALL SCHOOLS TAUGHT CHILDREN HOW TO FIND THEIR PASSIONS!

When I moved to Melbourne at twenty-two, I still had no idea what to do with my life. One of the first things I thought of after my 3am List experience was that I was passionate about travel. So perhaps a career in travel? I'd always loved to travel, so it seemed an obvious choice.

Off I went and I asked everyone I met if they knew anyone who worked in travel. I met as many people in the industry as I could, peppering them with questions about what they did, what they liked about it, what they didn't like, how they got into it, and so on.

This helped me understand the industry a bit better and gave me the confidence to literally knock on the door of an award-winning travel agent and explain that I was interested in a career in travel. Again, I offered to work for free to gain experience. I also suggested – a little bit cheekily – that they might give me a job one day if they decided I could add value to their business.

After two weeks of happily working for nothing in exchange for the opportunity and experience, they offered me a paid role! I stayed there for more than a year – and learnt lots – but the most important thing I learnt was that booking other people's travel didn't make me excited to drive to work on a Monday morning. I'd have to continue my search. It was a really valuable learning experience.

It wasn't long after, when I was almost boiling with frustration about not knowing what I wanted to do and struggling to find beautiful stationery products to set up my home office, that I finally landed on the idea of kikki.K. Combining my love of design with my love of Sweden and my deep passion for learning, I began building a brand and a business that I absolutely love. Through all the ups and downs, the energy I get from it is amazing. I believe everyone deserves to find their passion, whether it becomes a career or not, and embrace it as part of a life they love.

IF YOU LOVE WHAT YOU DO, YOU'VE ALREADY WON HALF THE BATTLE. AND IF YOU DON'T LOVE WHAT YOU DO, NOW'S THE TIME TO START EXPLORING.

Are you in a similar situation to the one I was in? Are you unsure about what you want to do or if your planned career or direction in life is actually for you?

Above all, I encourage you to work for free or volunteer to get a true hands-on insight into whatever you think might be your thing. My experience is that nothing beats that. Now some people may see difficulties, like finding the time, finding a suitable organisation or finding someone to give you a chance. If your dream is strong enough, you will find a way.

I also encourage you to ask around and talk to people already in the area that interests you, to do a short course in that area, and read and research as much as you can.

Do you know someone who is already doing what you want to do? Or do you know of someone who's working in your dream role? If you're starting a business, do you know someone who has done something similar before, even if it's in a different area?

Ask people you admire how they got to where they are and if they can offer advice or support in any way. Seek out people who are doing what you want to do and offer to buy them lunch so you can ask your questions. Be specific. Many people have limited time so make sure you go with a list of prepared questions, take note of any learnings in a notebook, and be sure to show that you value and respect their time.

This was one of the most helpful actions I took when I was first starting kikki.K. I contacted people I admired, who had done what I wanted to do – set up a successful retail business – and asked to meet them for coffee. I asked specific questions: How did they get started? What were the challenges? What did they love about what they did? What would they do differently?

I literally filled my journal with notes and they almost always pointed me to other people who might be able to help. Many of these people became great supporters over the years. I always followed up with a handwritten thank-you card and an offer to help them in the future if the opportunity arose. Often people went well out of their way to help me. I believe this had a lot to do with the respect I showed for their time and an innate human instinct to help others who are trying to help themselves improve. You have to always think and act win-win – give something back to people who help you.

If you're interested in talking to a public figure or well-known person who may be hard to meet, then what can you read or learn about them elsewhere? So much of what I've learnt in business has been from books, seminars and courses. There is so much content and knowledge available to us today at the click of a button.

IF YOU'RE LOOKING FOR EVEN MORE INSPIRATION AND GUIDANCE ON THE IMPORTANCE OF DISCOVERING AND FOLLOWING YOUR PASSIONS, AND HOW YOU CAN LET THAT GUIDE YOU TOWARDS CREATING A LIFE YOU LOVE, I ENCOURAGE YOU TO LISTEN TO THE WONDERFUL CONVERSATION I HAD WITH ELLA MILLS, FOUNDER AND BRAND DIRECTOR OF DELICIOUSLY ELLA, ON MY PODCAST – 'YOUR DREAM LIFE WITH KRISTINA KARLSSON'. LISTEN TO HER INCREDIBLE EPISODE AND SUBSCRIBE ON APPLE PODCASTS, GOOGLE PODCASTS OR YOUR PREFERRED PODCAST STREAMING APP.

I AM CONVINCED THAT THE ONLY
THING THAT KEPT ME GOING WAS
THAT I LOVED WHAT I DID. YOU'VE
GOT TO FIND WHAT YOU LOVE ... AND
LOVE WHAT YOU DO.

- STEVE JOBS -
2005 STANFORD COMMENCEMENT ADDRESS

It's time to discover and write down your passions. To help you:

01 /

THERE'S A LOT YOU CAN DO TO EXPLORE AND DISCOVER YOUR PASSIONS. I'VE PUT TOGETHER A LIST OF QUESTIONS I LOVE TO ASK TO HELP GET YOU STARTED. DON'T BE AFRAID TO TRY NEW THINGS AND EXPLORE NEW PASSIONS TOO. IT'S SO VALUABLE TO CREATE A LIST (OR LISTS) OF THINGS YOU'RE PASSIONATE ABOUT. YOU CAN ADD TO IT, REVIEW IT AND EDIT IT OVER TIME. MAKE A START NOW TO HELP YOU DESIGN A LIFE YOU LOVE.

+ WHAT DO YOU LOVE TO DO?
+ WHAT DO YOU FIND YOURSELF DOING IN YOUR SPARE TIME?
+ WHAT DO YOU ALWAYS MAKE TIME FOR?
+ WHAT ARE YOU REALLY GOOD AT? WHAT ARE YOUR SKILLS AND STRENGTHS? WHAT'S YOUR MAGIC?
+ WHAT DO YOU CARE DEEPLY ABOUT?
+ THINK ABOUT TIMES WHEN YOU COMPLETELY LOST TRACK OF TIME – JUST ENJOYING WHAT YOU WERE DOING AND TOTALLY IN THE FLOW. WHAT WAS IT YOU WERE DOING? IS THERE SOMETHING IN THAT THAT COULD INDICATE A PASSION FOR YOU TO FOLLOW?

IF, WHEN ANSWERING THE QUESTIONS ABOVE, YOU THINK 'I GET LOST ON SOCIAL MEDIA FOR HOURS' – AND THAT HAPPENS TO MANY – THINK ABOUT WHAT IT IS THAT'S CAPTURING YOUR INTEREST. MAYBE IT'S YOUR INTEREST IN FOOD, FASHION OR HEALTH THAT MAKES YOU FIND IT COMPELLING? MAYBE IT'S THE WAY PEOPLE YOU FOLLOW ARE TRAVELLING, ARE FIT AND HEALTHY, OR ARE MAKING A DIFFERENCE IN THEIR WORLD? PONDER WHAT THIS MEANS FOR YOU AND IF THOSE THINGS SHOW WHAT YOU ARE PASSIONATE ABOUT.

I FIND THAT HAVING SOMEONE TO DISCUSS THESE EXERCISES WITH IS REALLY HELPFUL. TALKING THROUGH MY THOUGHTS OUT LOUD WITH SOMEONE I RESPECT AND TRUST OFTEN ADDS VALUE, HELPING MAKE IT CLEARER FOR ME. I RECOMMEND YOU DO THAT TOO.

02 /

NOW LOOK BACK OVER THIS LIST. HOW COULD YOU COMBINE YOUR
PASSIONS WITH YOUR STRENGTHS TO CREATE NEW DREAMS – TO BUILD A
FULFILLING NEW CAREER OR EXPLORE AN EXCITING NEW HOBBY OR SIDE
PROJECT? ADD ANY NEW DREAMS THAT SURFACE OUT OF THIS EXERCISE TO
YOUR 101 DREAMS LIST.

DISCOVER AND FOLLOW
YOUR PASSIONS

---

1 IF YOU LOVE WHAT YOU DO, YOU'VE ALREADY WON HALF THE BATTLE. AND IF YOU DON'T LOVE WHAT YOU DO, NOW'S THE TIME TO START EXPLORING

---

2 EMBRACING YOUR PASSIONS GIVES YOUR LIFE MEANING AND JOY

---

3 GET CREATIVE TO DISCOVER YOUR PASSIONS - WORK FOR FREE, ASK PEOPLE IN SIMILAR SITUATIONS, TAKE COURSES, LEARN AND STUDY

'TRY SOMETHING NEW –
YOU CAN DO IT!'

LISA LEMKE

I love my family, I love my home, I love writing and I love food. So I think that's one of the reasons why Lisa Lemke's pursuit of her dream life really inspires me. Somehow she's managed to combine all of this, and along the way she's created her dream life. Follow your passions!

I first met Lisa when I visited her beautiful backyard restaurant, Prostens Pizza, just out of my hometown of Falkenberg, on the west coast of Sweden. It was genuinely one of the best food experiences of my life. We'd ridden our bikes five kilometres through the lush forest to get there, then sat in her country garden for pre-dinner drinks with friends, surrounded by flowers, children and happy people as the sun slowly set on a balmy summer evening... The food was simple and amazing, and Lisa's hospitality was warm and genuine as she wandered around making people feel welcome. I asked her what her story was and, as you'll read ahead, you'll see how easy it was to be drawn to and inspired by the lovely Lisa, who is now a great friend.

Today, Lisa's face is instantly recognised by Swedish television viewers and thousands of online followers around the world. It's a long way from her childhood in rural Sweden where she dreamed of being a dairy farmer and filled notebook after notebook with potential names for all her future cows.

Later on, after a visit to the local newspaper, Lisa decided that perhaps writing was more to her taste, so she swapped her dream career from dairy farming to journalism.

'Crash, boom, bang – I fell totally in love with the world of words. Imagine writing for a living, every day and every year!' says Lisa.

Lisa's story is an important reminder that we all change and evolve over time, as do our dreams, and that embracing change and reimagining our dreams can lead us to shape a life that's just right for us.

Throughout her school years, Lisa talked herself into internships at newspapers and radio stations, and was blown away when she was offered a proper paying job at the local newspaper during the summer holidays. 'I was the proudest seventeen-year-old on earth!' she says.

On graduating high school, Lisa went on to study journalism at university, but the more she studied and the more she kept working part-time at the paper, the more strongly she felt that maybe – just perhaps – her dream career had changed. 'One big clue was that my interviews kept getting side-tracked into conversations about cinnamon rolls and barbecue techniques,' she says.

It was while she was studying in Edinburgh that the thunderbolt struck. 'I realised that I didn't have to choose between writing and my passion for food. I could simply write about food.'

Lisa took the plunge and set herself up as a freelance food writer. It took time, but slowly the pile of rejection emails turned to requests for her work. Her first cookbook followed and then she transferred her talents to television as host of the popular Swedish morning show, *My Kitchen*.

Lisa credits her success not only to hard work, but also to never (okay, almost never) being afraid of saying yes – even when she's not 100 per cent sure that she knows what to do and is scared to death. Unsurprisingly, one of her favourite sayings is: 'I have never tried that before, so I think I should definitely be able to do that' from the classic children's book, *Pippi Longstocking*, by Astrid Lindgren.

'I believe that once in a while we all need to try something that makes us a bit afraid or uncomfortable. For me, it was things like giving a speech in front of 1,000 people. Doing live TV for the first time. Or just taking on a new job or task I'd never done before.'

Today, Lisa lives in an old rectory in the countryside near Falkenberg with her husband, Marcus Nordgren (also a chef), their two children, two cats, lots of chickens and about 180,000 bees. Oh yes, and the award-winning restaurant, Prostens Pizza, in the garden. What happened?

Says Lisa, 'This is the interesting thing about dreaming. I'd always been a planner and I do still love lists and planning. What I now know is that it's also extremely important to make room for the unplanned, impulsive and spontaneous. Responding to the advertisement for the old rectory was when magic happened for us.'

Awards, international recognition and even a new prime-time television series are not the main thing for Lisa. She's followed her passions, reimagined her dreams as they've changed and has now dreamed up an idyllic life with her family that brings together all her passions. There are lessons there for all of us.

Let Lisa's story inspire you to discover and follow your passion. Take some time now while it's fresh in your mind to ponder on it and write down anything you've learnt that you could apply in your own life in your notebook or journal.

ALWAYS REMEMBER, YOU HAVE

WITHIN YOU THE STRENGTH, THE

PATIENCE, AND THE PASSION

TO REACH FOR THE STARS TO

CHANGE THE WORLD.

- HARRIET TUBMAN -

LET YOUR PASSIONS GUIDE YOUR DREAMS

Understanding that you are in control of your life is very empowering. It's an exciting moment when you realise that the only person who can create change and turn your dreams into reality is you. But yes, it can be slightly scary because you realise that it's up to you to make things happen for yourself.

This takes a bit of getting used to, so it's important to give yourself time to do that, but when you do it's the most liberating feeling. It means that whatever you dream, whatever you are determined to make happen, you can. It's up to you to make your dreams come true.

Writing everything down and revisiting my lists on a regular basis is the best way I know to keep my passions front of mind and my dreams close to my heart. It's so you're ready to act when you meet someone who can inspire or mentor you. And it's so you can recognise opportunities that will help you transform your dreams into something tangible.

Having a good idea of what you're most passionate about is a great way to develop a stronger sense of purpose towards creating your dream life. These things are unique to you so understanding them is a great place to start when planning to make your dream life a reality.

Why? Because when you are dreaming, setting goals or making big decisions, having a clear understanding and simple list of your passions – in writing – keeps you focused on what is truly important and simplifies your decisions. Your dream life is very likely to be one where you are guided strongly by the things you are passionate about.

If you like, you can dig deeper into this important process by reading the other books in this series.

I've filled this book with all sorts of ideas and approaches that helped me start kikki.K and that I still use today for everything that is most precious in my life, including my family and friends. I find that this approach works across all the different parts of my life, helping to bring them together, and to open up new and exciting possibilities for an even more fulfilling future. I wish you all the strength and inspiration in taking hold of your passions on your journey to creating your dream life.

WHAT NOW?

'IF YOU ARE WORKING ON SOMETHING
EXCITING THAT YOU REALLY CARE ABOUT,
YOU DON'T HAVE TO BE PUSHED. THE
VISION PULLS YOU.'

— STEVE JOBS —

SHARE YOUR DREAMS AND ACHIEVEMENTS
WITH ME AND INSPIRE OTHERS…

You read earlier that my biggest dream is to inspire and empower 101 million people around the world to dream.

I'm so passionate about this. I know we can create a profoundly positive impact and send waves of change and inspiration around the world this way. Please join in the conversation with me and with our global community of like-minded dreamers by following and sharing via @kristinakikkik and @kikki.K – using #kikkiKDreamLife and #101MillionDreamers.

Connect more deeply and learn more at www.kikki-k.com/dreamlife

Our Dream Life portal, for you and our global online dream community, features a curated selection of content, tools, products and resources to support you on your dreaming journey. Join our global movement and discover a world of inspiration, including my *Your Dream Life Starts Here* book and accompanying journal, my 'Your Dream Life with Kristina Karlsson' podcast, workshops, free audio guides, worksheets and so much more at www.kikki-k.com/dreamlife.

Subscribe to 'Your Dream Life with Kristina Karlsson' podcast

If you enjoyed the inspiring stories in this book, be sure to subscribe to my podcast 'Your Dream Life with Kristina Karlsson' on Apple Podcasts, Google Podcasts or your preferred podcast streaming app.

Inspire others to dream...

And if you've found this book and process valuable, help send ripples of possibility around the globe by recommending or gifting a copy of this book or others in the series to anyone you know who'll benefit.

And of course, you can find more inspiration, tools, content and products to inspire you to continue living your dream life at kikki-k.com.

YOUR DREAM READING
AND RESOURCE LIST

+ BERESFORD, BRUCE, DIR. *MAO'S LAST DANCER*. 2009; PADDINGTON, NSW: GREAT SCOTT PRODUCTIONS, FILM.
+ CUNXIN, LI. *MAO'S LAST DANCER*. MELBOURNE: PENGUIN VIKING, 2003.
+ CUNXIN, LI. *THE PEASANT PRINCE*. MELBOURNE: PENGUIN VIKING, 2007.
+ HUFFINGTON, ARIANNA. *THRIVE: THE THIRD METRIC TO REDEFINING SUCCESS AND CREATING A LIFE OF WELL-BEING, WISDOM, AND WONDER*. NEW YORK: HARMONY BOOKS, 2014.
+ LEMKE, LISA. *THE SUMMER TABLE*. NEW YORK: STERLING EPICURE, 2015.
+ LEMKE, LISA. *THE WINTER TABLE*. NEW YORK: STERLING EPICURE, 2017.
+ MILLS, ELLA. *DELICIOUSLY ELLA: THE PLANT-BASED COOKBOOK*. LONDON: YELLOW KITE, 2018.
+ MILLS, ELLA. *DELICIOUSLY ELLA: THE PODCAST*. PODCAST AUDIO. HTTPS://PODCASTS.APPLE.COM/AU/PODCAST/DELICIOUSLY-ELLA-THE-PODCAST/ID1428704212
+ RUBIN, GRETCHEN. *BETTER THAN BEFORE: WHAT I LEARNED ABOUT MAKING AND BREAKING HABITS - TO SLEEP MORE, QUIT SUGAR, PROCRASTINATE LESS, AND GENERALLY BUILD A HAPPIER LIFE*. NEW YORK: BROADWAY BOOKS, 2015.
+ RUBIN, GRETCHEN. *THE HAPPINESS PROJECT*. NEW YORK: HARPERCOLLINS PUBLISHERS INC, 2015.
+ RUBIN, GRETCHEN. *OUTER ORDER, INNER CALM: DECLUTTER AND ORGANIZE TO MAKE MORE ROOM FOR HAPPINESS*. NEW YORK: HARMONY, 2019.
+ RUBIN, GRETCHEN. *HAPPIER PODCAST*. PODCAST AUDIO. HTTPS://GRETCHENRUBIN.COM/PODCASTS/